PRAISE

"Sage Taylor Kingsley's words hold the mark of the true mystic.
These magic words know how to dance! In the tradition of Rumi
and Hafiz, each piece ignites a sacred aliveness deep within us.
The entire collection invites us to open our hearts
more fully, join the divine stage,
and whirl again. This book is a jewel."
~ Chelan Harkin, Author of *The Prophetess:
The Return of* The Prophet *from the Voice of the Divine Feminine*

"One does not fall into the words of Sage Taylor Kingsley's poetry—
her words fall into you and become the seasons of awakening.
It's like holding your mouth open and letting the whole blue
sky fall in, in the Springtime … or letting strawberries burn
your lips red in the Summer.
This collection is not a seed in the garden of the soul,
it is the whole forest.
I found myself in that forest."
~ Kendall Rosenberg M.A.,
Author of *All the Candles I Light for Myself, I Light for You*

"Sage's poetry has got an element of Rupi Kaur but is more grown up and sexy. More magical. More joyful!"
~ E. M. McConnell,
Author of *Of Swans and Stars,* and *The Sunset Sovereign*

"Sage's stirring words inspire, arouse, soothe, and surprise, speaking to us of self-love, sensuality, natural delights, and sacred connections. As a lover of carnal pleasures, she weaves a sizzling web of words around you, while as a profoundly mystic poet, she uses rhythm, repetition, rhyme, and a transcendent grasp of language and lyricism to bring us closer to the divine.

"Turn to this book whenever you need cheering up, grounding down, or expansion of your soul. You will love every page."
~ Lanette Sweeney, Author of *What I Should Have Said: A Poetry Memoir about Losing a Child to Addiction*

"This brilliant treasure is a wellspring for all souls in communion with the sacred bliss of the Divine (who may be a She!). Drink from the chalice of Sage's wisdom and imbibe the beauty of eternal love within the truth of poetic inspiration."
~ Julia Lindsay Carroll
Author of *Star Ride: Poems for Awakening Starseeds*

"Sage Taylor Kingsley is clearly smitten, truly surrendered to the one
voice that sings all other voices. She knows the source of the hymns
that unlocked in the breasts of Hafiz and Rumi so many centuries ago,
and she harmonizes with their echo. Her passion is palpable.
If you wish to be spun in rhythm with the heartbeat
of the universe, dance with her words.
They will dervish you into the sky,
into your own inner sanctuary,
inviting a deep remembering."
~ Cit Ananda, DDiv., author of *When Silence Speaks:
Messages from the Heart*

"I am not usually a fan of poetry books, but this one: Wow!
Every piece made this adrenaline-fueled speed reader slow
down, savor each poem and line slowly and reverently,
as if dining at the finest gourmet restaurant. Sage is a walking,
writing, embodiment of the divine feminine, highly drunk on love,
and, in my opinion, a modern-day Hafiz and, dare I say it, Rumi.
The word 'goddess' gets tossed around too much these days,
but in her case, I would not hesitate to use the G word to describe her.
Her love of life, every inch of it, pours from every poem, every page.

"Please read this book. At the very least you
will get a contact high—and share in her intoxication.
For that reason, you may not want to read or listen
to it while driving or operating heavy machinery!"
~ Scott Grace, Author of *Mindful Masculinity,
Teach Me How to Love,* and other books

"Sage Taylor Kingsley is a mystic poet of extraordinarily powerful love and passion for the Divine. She has the unique desire and ability to hold her reader in the same way that the Divine holds creation. She writes, 'Who holds the ancient stones/in the silent beds/holds us.'

"Every poem overflows with spiritual gifts. Her poems are incantatory, rhythmic, evocative. Delightful and compelling, ecstatic and loving.

"I adore her musical alliteration and assonance, and I find many of her poems bold, wild, playful, and hilarious! She is living proof that spirituality does not have to always be somber and serious! Sage is an inventive craftswoman with a wide variety of poetic forms, styles, ideas, and approaches, from sacred to sexy—and the imagery!

"I will always want more from Sage, as she opens her heart to us, expanding our joy in the revelation of our own divine spirit in the world."
~ Achali Hall, a.k.a. Susan Rankin, Artist (fineartamerica.com), poet, author of *To Whom Do I Bow*

SAGE TAYLOR KINGSLEY

Beautiful Late Bloomer

Passionate Poetry & Mystic Musings

YONI-VERSE BOOK 1

Copyright © 2026 by Taylor Esta Kingsley.
All rights reserved. First Edition.
Published and printed in the United States of America.

This book is the property of Taylor Esta Kingsley. No part of this book may be reproduced, stored within a retrieval system, or transmitted in any form or by any means without the author's written permission except for the use of quotations in a book review, cited appropriately.

Paperback ISBN   978-0-9963202-1-4
Ebook ISBN   978-0-9963202-2-1

Book Cover Design and Interior Formatting by 100Covers:
https://100covers.com/?ref=194
Use coupon SAGE20 for 20% off a gorgeous cover.

Published by Yoni-Verse Press

https://linktr.ee/sagetheprosperousgoddess
Editing, Ghostwriting, and Poetry Curation Services: www.SageforYourPage.com

"First Words" originally published in *Self-Caring* by Michelle Peck (2022).
"Find the Pool" originally published in *The Destiny Designer* by Lauren Perotti (2016).
"Love Dancer" with heart rays designed by Sage Taylor Kingsley and Mark Goddard.

Author photos by Forest Goddard SunLanternMedia.com

Many other poems herein were originally published on Sage's Substack blog/museletter at:
https://sagepoetess.substack.com (museletter)
https://www.substack.com/@sagepoetess (bio)
Contact: sagepoetess@gmail.com

Library of Congress Control Number: 2025925851 (print)

DEDICATION

Dedicated with all my love to:

My mothers
My muses
My magic

CONTENTS

PRAISE ii
DEDICATION ix
PREFACE 1

PART I
BLESSING

Come, Come, Rumi 7
First Words. 10
Find the Pool 11
The Job, the Joy, of the Poet. 12
Empty Cup 13
At the Cup of the Divine 14
The Inner Baptism. 16
Write a Thousand Poems 18
breath wave 19
They Come Bidden and Unbidden 20
Master, Pray Tell Me. 22
Soaked with Words. 24
The Many Moods 25
Beloved, How Long Have You Loved Me? 26
When You Listen to the Silence 27
A Sacred Eavesdropping 28
I Tried to Send These Poems Back to Source 30
When Rumi Speaks 31
Job Description: Invisible Counselor 32
God Is in the Little Things 34
Spiritual Rap #1: "ReJoySing Truth". 36

PART II
BLOOMING

Bloom 41
I'm Every Woman 42
Permission Granted 43
Dating in My 50s 44
Allowing 48
Triple Goddess Kiss 49
Arc of Creation 50
She Is 51
Big Bang Blooming 52
To Love with Hearts Wide Open 54
I Won't Groan Up 55
She Is Breathing 56
There's Beauty in This Booty 58
Happy Mirthday! 59
When I Am 60 60
Tick Tock 61
Through the Eyes of Beauty 62
Legs? Or Legacy? 64
The Ghost in You 65
When I Am an Old Woman 66
I Saw God Sitting on a Bench 68
Bloom and Shine! 70
Flower Power 71
Yummilicious 72
Aging 73
Ageless 74
When Was the Last Time . . . ? 75
Writing through the Ages 76
The Treasure in the Mirror 77
Your Words Are Your Wonder 78
graysquishyoldishsoftstrongkissablefuckableGORGEOUS 80
YOU: A Love Poem 81
YONIverse 82

PART III
BLISSING

Bask	87
The Invitation	88
Poets Sure Know How to Throw Great Orgies (Wanna Come?)	90
Peach Sunrises	91
Deeper and Deeper	92
See the Love in All Things	94
Efflorescence	95
I Will No Longer Tolerate Itchy Sweaters!	96
go ahead, be self-bliss	98
Once	99
A Liminal Luminosity	100
when did we forget we are animals?	101
The Heart's Camera	102
You Are Forever a Mother	104
Love Activation #1	106
Cracking Open the Heart Egg	107
She Is Remembering	108
Sturdy Star Stuff	110
The Ecstasy of Being	113
On the Altar of Her Becoming	114
The Right One for You	116
Softly, a Love Note	118
Eternity in Your Eyes	119
Dancing Love Bubbles	120
pat pat pat	122
We Interrupt This Poetry Book to Bring You an Important Message from Your Creator	123
Worship the Hands	124
I No Longer Pray	126
As If	128
Just. One. More.	129
When Does It Ever End?	130

ABOUT THE POET 132
CONNECT WITH SAGE 134

PREFACE

> *"Different trees bear fruit in different seasons.
> If you're looking around and feeling behind because others
> are blooming, just remember, you're a different kind
> of tree. Your season will come."*
> ~ Julie Fratantoni, PhD

My first poem was about love.

I was nine. The early glimmerings and shimmerings of the woman I would become already were shining within me, and in my favorite playthings: words.

I've been penning poetry, as well as writing songs, essays, personal growth courses and books, for half a century. And now, finally—finally, at the age of 60!—I am getting my debut collection of poems out to the world. I feel as if I've been forty-two weeks pregnant with poems for a very, very long time, so this is a joyous birth indeed.

I had been writing a poem here and there, maybe one a month, from age 9-56.

And then, the holy floodgates opened.

On Spring Equinox 2021, I woke up with an inner voice stating calmly: "I'm going to write a poem a day for a year." *What?!* I thought. *A year? That's CRAZY!* Then I intuitively felt into it. *Ah. Yes. I will.* It was as if I had signed a soul contract. All I needed to do was physically catch up to the energetic commitment.

And I did. Those 365 poems will come in another book, but this collection—first in the Yoni-Verse series—shaped itself around themes of love and awakening. Here you will find poems on aging with grace and gratitude; softness and sensuality; seeing the beauty and feeling the magic all around you … and in the mirror. May these sacred messages remind you of the remarkable power of words as portals, as healing balms, and as pathways to peace and joy and hope.

"Yoni-Verse" popped into my head because … I'll tell you a secret … shhhh …

My yoni writes poems.

Well, OK, maybe not literally. I haven't tried putting a pen in there, but I'm pretty sure no matter how many kegels I do … LOL :) Here's what I mean by: "My yoni writes poems."

My massive creative expansion and explosion that began that March morning coincided exactly with a sexual reawakening. The second chakra governs creativity and sexuality, as well as playfulness. After the end of a 23-year marriage, the ink was dry on my divorce papers in October 2020, and I felt dried up, too. I had allowed my sexual self to go into a coma, and when I realized this, I made a conscious choice to revive that part of me—not only my body, but my juicy aliveness. These poems drip with amrita, holy waters imbued with the energy of ecstasy in all forms.

This sacred flood has continued daily now for almost five years. Nearly every day, I write a poem, sometimes many. (The maximum in one day was thirty-one!)

I see creativity on a spectrum from human to divine. I have noticed that the MOST beautiful creations don't arise from my head or even heart; they beam and stream into me, landing in my heart and my hands instantly. Perfectly. Easily.

For the word weavings that flow into me so effortlessly, I am an astonished recipient. I humbly take divine dictation. I feel those poems come from Source (God, Goddess, Creator, or dare I say, The Yoniverse).

Some pieces herein feel like a conversation, with the divine voice in *italics,* and my human one regular text. By the way, I don't believe any of this makes me special. I believe *all* art originates in Source, and we all have that capacity. Our task is to clear out the static in the pipeline. I am so happy to be a clear straw for the Great Cosmic Chocolate Milkshake!

Others—crafted by my inquisitive mind and healing heart to reflect my life experience and express my voice—can benefit from percolation and revision, adding another brushstroke here and there. For the creations that do feel like "mine," that my head shapes and my heart gushes, I am deepening into the value of receiving feedback, reading word art from other poets (both Dead Poets and Live), and also collaborating with others, in collective cocreation. Substack is so wonderful for this! I feel incredibly seen, heard, appreciated, applauded, and lauded there.

It was thrilling to see this note on Substack go viral!

Come play with me and with words at:
sagepoetess.substack.com

I get inspiration all sorts of places. In the bath. Sitting outside in nature. When making love. While driving the car. Even from dreams.

I live, eat, love, breathe, drink, and dream poetry!

May these words of love ignite you and delight you.

And remember:

It's never too late to bloom and shine! ❤ ***Sage***

PART I

BLESSING

Come, Come, Rumi ...

Come, come, Rumi ...
Come, come, Hafiz ...
Come speak to me and through me.

Come whisper in my inner ear
of love's sacred song.

Come whisper in my heart
of being loved by the Beloved
of being Love.

Come pour the sweetest of wines
onto my parched tongue.
Come fill my cup.
Come fill my soul up.

Beautiful one!
We are here, yes, you hear us, yes.
But know this, beloved:
We but led you to the cup.
You picked it up.
We but showed you how light it is
for it is made of light.

The Great One who fills our cups
fills yours
fills all vessels
always
with the holiest honeyed nectars

*with that one wine that makes you drunk with love
and truth and beauty
yet causes neither stagger nor stupor.*

*Yes, we could hand you your cup
but you don't need us to do so anymore.
Now it is your turn.
Now it is your time.
To show others how to find their cups
To help them remember how easy it is,
how natural, how magnificent,
to simply pick up their cup
that is always, already filled,
always all ready to quench
that thirst they could never name.*

*So go, dear one, go.
Go, all beloveds.
Pick up the cup.*

*Drink
Swallow
And shine.*

When the sun rises, drink.

When the birds sing, drink.

When the lovers touch, drink.

When the children laugh, drink.

When the body moves, drink.

When the heart beats, drink.

When the lungs breathe, drink.

Beautiful Late Bloomer

When the breeze blows, drink.

When the moon glows, drink.

Drink and be drunk on the wonder of life.

Be the hand that pours.
Be the vessel.
Be the wine.
Be the warmth.
Be the euphoria.

Be the love, beloved.

Be love.
Be love.
Be love.

First Words

Let your first words
> from pen and lips
> be: "Thank you"
> be: "I love you"
> be: "I am blessed."

The day embraces you
as you embrace the day.

Find the Pool

*Find the pool of infinite wisdom within your own heart.
Drink deep of the nectar you find there.
Fill yourself with the Light that has no end.*

The Job, the Joy, of the Poet

The job of the poet
is to take all the pain and pleasure
All the chaos and clarity
All the struggle and beauty

Of being human

Of being alive

Of being here on this Earth
distill it into words
that make your heart gasp in recognition:
"Oh! Ah! Yes! That is my experience!
How do you know it, how do you know me so well
when we have never met?"

The joy of the poet
Is to receive these glowing, singing wordsongs
And to quickly capture them like caged birds
Then let them fly free again.

Empty Cup

I am the empty cup, thirsting:
"Where is my water?"

Here, beloved, have wine.

At the Cup of the Divine

At the cup of the Divine,
I sip
and sip
and slurp
and guzzle
And somehow my cup
is always full.
Do you feel thirsty?
Is your joycup empty?
Hold it up to the Sun,
and it will be filled.
Hold it up to the Moon,
and it will be filled.
Hold it up to the Stars,
and it will be filled.
Hold it up to your own precious heart,
and it will be filled.
In fact, you can pour it all onto the sweet parched Earth
as an offering,
And still, look! it will be filled.
Or, if you like, my friend,
Hold it out to me and
let me fill your cup from mine.
It but takes a recognition,
an understanding
that you deserve your every thirst quenched,
a willingness to receive

And even if you have lost your faith
Just hold out your cup
And let the universe prove to you
again
and again
that your source is endless.
Drink.

- Inspired by Hafiz, Rumi, and akasha

At the cup of the divine

Sage Taylor Kingsley

The Inner Baptism

A benediction
Reach inward
Tap the pool of your holiest
Water
(yes, in your heart, you know that secret place
so well … shhhh … don't tell me where)

Now send ripples through
Every liquid molecule
Comprising this
Ocean of Love
Disguised in human shape

A sacrament
Your elixir
Ever-flowing
Originating from the
Original blessing

Now hear how this communion
Reveals how connected you already
Are to all that is, to all that is
Love

The inner baptism

Fountain of youth

Annoint your brow

Beautiful Late Bloomer

Open your inner window to infinity

Now notice how that
Heavenly waterfall
Rains blessings
And rainbows
Behind your eyes

dip
and
dunk
and
dive
and
drink

Christ turned water into wine.
God turned water into you.

SAGE TAYLOR KINGSLEY

Write a Thousand Poems

*Write a thousand poems
and a thousand thousand more
and still, not one utterance
can ever come close to describing
the beauty of Creation,
the generosity of your Creator.*

*But try, oh, yes, dearest heart.
Do try.*

breath wave

presence contentment gratitude breath desire intensity power breath
somatic sensation scintillation softness smiling breath
achievement satisfaction fulfillment breath
inspiration creation celebration breath
pleasure happiness joy breath
ecstasy bliss elation breath

ecstasy bliss elation breath
pleasure happiness joy breath
inspiration creation celebration breath
achievement satisfaction fulfillment breath
somatic sensation scintillation softness smiling breath
presence contentment gratitude breath desire intensity power breath

Sage Taylor Kingsley

They Come Bidden and Unbidden

They come bidden and unbidden
like lovers in the night
sought and seeking
Who is seeking whom?

I lie in bed, head softly still on my pillow
and suddenly
in
they
stream
like technicolor dreams in sense-a-round sound
"pay attention" they whisper
and my sleepy eyes open just enough
to
grab a
pen

They come bidden and unbidden
like unexpected flowers popping up
between sidewalk cracks
all the more glorious for their surprising
locales and quiet moments
just
bringing me, you
alive

Beautiful Late Bloomer

They come bidden and unbidden
like memories
like desires
like treasures
always mysteries
always golden, mine
to be mined

Some I keep close to me, hidden
Some I have to sprinkle on the world like silvery rainbow confetti
Celebrating the marriage of mind and soul

They come bidden and unbidden

Will you see them?
Will you pay attention?
Will you hear their whispers
when they stealthily, boldly
kiss their magic upon the eyelids of
your heart?

Sage Taylor Kingsley

Master, Pray Tell Me

Master, pray tell me this:
Are you in the Air?
For when I stand atop the mountain
and the wind whips my face alive
and my hair dances like snakes,
When I feel the breeze's rustle, the forest's leaves like soft hands
When I hear the birdsong and my own breast cascades open,
I am convinced that you are Air.

Yes, beloved, I am Air.
Purity
Clarity
I am vision and breath and movement.

Master, pray tell me this:
Are you in the Fire?
For when I gaze into the dancing flames
and dragons and lovers and prancing horses appear,
When my bones and skin glow warmly
and my pulse quickens with passion
When I see Sun's glow arising, asetting
and I come alive again with the Light,
I am convinced that you are Fire.

Yes, beloved, I am Fire.
Power
Energy
I am radiance and vibrance and intensity.

Beautiful Late Bloomer

Master, pray tell me this:
Are you in the Water?
For when I catch raindrops on my cheeks and snowflakes on my tongue,
When I float and swim, buoyant and graceful as a mermaid,
When I quench my thirsts and see the clouds part to reveal the Moon aglow over and within the Sea,
I am convinced that you are Water.

Yes, beloved, I am Water.
Flowing
Storming
I am river and mist and mystery.

Master, pray tell me this:
Are you in the Earth?
For when I smell the dark sweet soil,
When the dirt beneath my fingernails makes me smile
and stomp and sway and drum,
When my soul is in my soles and Gaia's beauty
ecstasizes my mouth and eyes with seed and flower and fruit,
I am convinced that you are Earth.

Yes, beloved, I am Earth.
Pleasuring
Treasuring
I am strength and solidity and firmness.

Master, pray tell me this:
Where are you not?

Sage Taylor Kingsley

Soaked with Words

drip.
at first a little dribble
drop.
first word splashes on my forehead
drizzle.
better grab that pen
downpour.
can't write fast enough
deluge.
afloat a lake of glimmering poetry
drenched.
the baptism never ends

The Many Moods

The splendor of starlight
The mirth of moonlight
The sauciness of sunlight

The tenacity of tundra
The gaiety of grasslands
The despair of desert

The raucousness of raindrops
The slowness of snowflakes
The ripeness of rainbows

The momentousness of mountains
The jubilance of jungles
The surprise of the seas

The wisdom of the woods
The frolicking of flowers
The merriness of mushrooms

The lavishness of lightning
The naughtiness of nightfall
The dutifulness of dawn

God sure is moody,
Isn't She?

Sage Taylor Kingsley

Beloved, How Long Have You Loved Me?

Beloved, how long have you loved me?

How long have the stars been in the sky?

Beloved, how can I show my love to you?

How do Moon and Sun love one another?

Beloved, how is it that these words of love never end?

From ocean to cloud and back again,
Our love songs, in word, in dance, in play,
Will always be praising
Hearts open.

When You Listen to the Silence

when you listen to the silence
you hear the music of the mystery

when you listen to the silence
you hear the teachings of the trees

when you listen to the silence
you hear the messages of truth

when you listen to the silence
you hear the whispers of Creation

when you listen to the silence
the universe
is always singing you
a love song

A Sacred Eavesdropping

Head says:
Who am I?
What's going on?
Where am I heading?
When will I ever get there?
And why am I taking so long?!

Body says:
Breathe.

Heart says:
Love.

Head says:
Oh, you shush! That's all you ever want to talk about.
Can't you see I'm having an existential crisis over here!?
I need proof! I need ANSWERS! I need—

Soul says:
You already have the answer to every question.
Did you hear what Love just said?
Love is who you are. Love is the only choice, the only thing that matters,
the only song, the rest is static. Love is both your road and destination.
You will arrive on Love's time, beloved.
In fact, you already have.

Head says:
Ah! Ahhhh.
What a relief!
Thank you!

Heart says:
(Smile)

Sage Taylor Kingsley

I Tried to Send These Poems Back to Source

I tried to send these poems back to Source,
fearing that I am an unworthy delivery vehicle
yet they came back to me, even stronger than ever,

I tried to claim that I am too busy with worldly affairs
too tired, too run down by health concerns, too limited of resources
to do what needs to be done
and yet they continue to come to me, brighter and wider,
lighter and wiser, bolder and louder than ever.

I tried to hold these words inside my own soul's mouth,
and yet they spill from me every time I breathe.

So please excuse me if my hands drip poems into your ears, beloved
for that is all they are capable of doing at this point,
and if you stand near me, your heart may open, entranced in ecstatic awe
and the One who drips these poems onto our hearts
and drops these words into our souls
will only nod and
smile.

When Rumi Speaks

when Rumi speaks
my soul listens
and my fingers get busy

when Hafiz urges
my holiness dances
and my spinning resumes

when Gibran teaches
my heart eye unfurls
and my mind knows everything
(yet nothing)

when the holy ones meet
I pour them wine
they tell me: drink!

what will you do
when they speak
to you?

Job Description: Invisible Counselor

When I'm all flown up
I want to be an Invisible Counselor
A Spirit Guide
A Muse

My team:
Henry and Anais
Mae and Maya
Rumi Hafiz Gibran
Samuel and Benjamin
Ursula and Mary
Douglas and Isaac
Wendell and Walt
Hildegard and Pablo
Emily and Rainer
and of course Dr. Seuss

Pop into writers' dreams
Whisper poetry on the breeze

Nudge them: Time to write, right now, write now,
share a giggle

Orchestrate synchronicities—
the book
the writer
the teacher
the scene
the gasp
the tingles
the magic

~ Inspired by Napoleon Hill's Think and Grow Rich
And David Fealkoff's Creating Possibilities
(which I had the pleasure of editing)

Sage Taylor Kingsley

God Is in the Little Things

God is in the little things.

Yes, yes, She is also in the great things.
The majestic redwoods soaring,
The clouds drifting, the rainbows.
The heroic acts. The medical miracles.
The "Eureka!"s. The births.

But God is also in the hand that stirs the soup.
She is also in the feet that trudge at 3 a.m.
to soothe the crying babe.

He is also in every petal of every flower
and every sigh following every scent
that makes your soul smile.

God is in the simple messages we deliver with presence.
The "Thank you"s. The "I love you so much"s.
The "I am here for you"s.

Yes, yes, They are in the cathedrals and mosques,
the temples and mountaintops. And God, of course,
attends the funerals, the weddings, the graduations,
the rites of passage.

But God is also here in those unsung moments,
in the unseen quiet kindnesses, in the hands that hold,
the lips that kiss, in every act of pleasure.

Beautiful Late Bloomer

And God is right here, below you, around you.
Do you see the tiny spider, the ant, the ladybug?
Can you hear them softly breathing?
They too have mouths to feed, and journeys to take.

God is there.

And look further.
God is in that plain grey rock we call dull,
as well as the sparkling gems.
God is in that weed, and in the broken seashells, too.

God is in the little things, the hidden things,
the quiet things, the broken things.

God is in these little words.

And God is in you.

Spiritual Rap #1: "ReJoySing Truth"

You are a piece of God
You are at peace with God
You are Infinity
Divinity
at ease with God.

You are a ray of Light
You are a bay of Light
You are Brilliant
and Resilient
on the way of Light.

You are the voice of Truth
You make the choice of Truth
You are Courageously
Outrageously
Rejoicing Truth!

You are the art of Love
Forever part of Love
You remember,
Shining Ember,
You're the Heart of Love.

You live a sacred Vow
Your Words of Light, your How
In all your glimmerings
'N shimmerings,
Your power: NOW!

See, hear, and feel Sage
rapping/reciting this poem at:

https://www.youtube.com/watch?v=L-8xrjaB4p8

Or search Youtube.com "Spiritual Rap #1 Sage Taylor Kingsley
The Prosperous Goddess"

PART II

BLOOMING

Bloom

Flowers bloom.
Not because someone may happen by and admire them.
Flowers bloom because they are designed to
To evolve and expand
To reach toward the light
To attract helpful beings
And because, I am quite certain, it feels good.
They bloom at just the right time.
Flowers bloom attending only to nature's clock, embedded in their every cell and leaf and petal.
Ask yourself, you lovely miracle of Earth and Sky:
How can I bloom today?
This week?
This month?
This year?
Always?
What will blooming feel like?
How will I know when I'm blooming?
And if you don't feel ready to bloom yet, if you're not getting any divine nudges to stretch and open and show off your bright, majestic gorgeousness, could it be that it's not quite time yet? That you're gathering resources for building, for bolstering, for blooming?
If you were a flower, what kind would you be?
Because you are, you know.
And I can see your bloomin' loveliness from here, root, stem, leaf, fruit, flower, every stage and age of your youness is pure magic and wild grace.

SAGE TAYLOR KINGSLEY

I'm Every Woman

inside this 50-something
lives the giddiness of a teenager
the libido of a 20-something
the vitality of a 30-something
the confidence of a 40-something
the wisdom of a 60-something
and the compassion of a 70-something

Permission Granted

I don't need permission from my parents
my friends or followers
my exes, my children, or society
to receive pleasure …

The only one whose permission I need is my own.

Repeat after me:

**I give myself full permission
to receive pleasure, always.**

Sage Taylor Kingsley

Dating in My 50s

dating in my 50s
post-divorce
I never online dated before
what IS this strange world of swiping and sexting
and ghosting and texting?

goodness gracious

the last time I dated I was 33
a lot has changed in 24 years
and most of it, within ME

dating in my 50s
is so much less important
so much less rushed
so much less urgent
so much less clear
so much less pressured

in my 30s
it was all about finding The One
living together
getting engaged
getting married
having babies
buying house(s)
not necessarily in that order

Beautiful Late Bloomer

it was all about long-term and forever
yet, of course, it seldom works out that way
(did you know that of the 48% of married couples
who DON'T divorce, only 3% of them are both very happy
with their relationship? that means that, if we define
success in marriage = both partners are very satisfied,
and the marriage lasts, and we do the math,
literally 1% of marriages succeed!)

so maybe there's something wrong with our essential assumptions
as individuals looking for love, and as a society

maybe it's ok to be a serial monogamist
and to honor the arc that every relationship has

maybe it's perfect to stay as long as it feels wonderful
and if you know you've given it your best shot
and then to pay attention and follow the signs

maybe it's perfect to consciously uncouple
and set one another free for the new loves right for you
NOW

because who you were 5 or 12 or 23 years ago
is not who you are today

dating and finding and nurturing love in my 50s
is less about looking toward creating a future together
and more about being present with each other
in the bliss of this moment

it's less of the panicky: "I don't want to make a mistake!"
and more of the: "I trust my intuition now, I trust my heart,
I trust my body"

it's less of the: "This HAS to be our forever love, this is IT, hallelujah!"
and more of: "This is so beautiful and is exactly what I want now,
and I am going to go with it and flow with it for however long
it continues to delight me, satisfy my needs and desires,
put smiles on my face, vavavoom in my loins,
and sweetness in my life"

every age and stage of love has its place, its purpose, its passion

I for one am relieved to be able to focus less on creating a family
and more on creating—elating—celebrating a harmony

less "where is this going?"
and more "how is this flowing?"

less "does he love me?"
and more "do I love this?"

do I love the way I feel when I'm with him
and when we're apart?

do I love the energy we share?

does this relationship support the fullness of who I am
and the magic of who I am becoming?

do I feel safe, seen, heard, met, and cherished?

do I feel inspired and uplifted by my partner, and by us?

does this enhance my life
and advance my personal growth and spiritual evolution
(rather than distract and detract with drama)?

we get to just focus on pleasure and play and presence
(with no worries about pregnancy, no need for condoms,
no care about what others may think or wish or judge
because we have the maturity to be in our own power,
and, hell yes, heaven yes, I'm going to moan and scream
and squeal as loudly as I want!)

I'm 100% animal and 100% tantric
and everything in the middle

I am learning to embrace and be embraced
as a sensual, sexual, social, and sacred being
as never before

and now is the perfect time.

Sage Taylor Kingsley

Allowing

I decided to enjoy
this time of my life
by allowing myself to have
the time of my life.

Triple Goddess Kiss

Who is that in the mirror?

She paused
Still half expecting the raven-haired sultry Maiden who had zero clue
how traffic-stopping gorgeous she was

She gazed
Still half expecting the smooth-skinned, ever-so-competent Mother
who so loved to dance, overgiver, life bringer

She smiled
Fully greeting the calm, courageous, outraged, outrageous Crone, she
of flowy silver moonlocks, rider of Dragons, scribe and seer

She winked
And all three muses laughed:
a giggle   a chuckle   a cackle
And blew her back

A kiss.

SAGE TAYLOR KINGSLEY

Arc of Creation

I dream.
I laugh.
I wonder.
I pray.
I sing.
I grieve.
I heal.
I caress.
I receive.
I comfort.
I climax.
I collapse.
I write.
I exult.
I surrender.
I wait.

I follow an invisible arc of creation,
cast in my life sky by an unseen hand.

~ Inspired by Anais Nin

She Is

Alluring
Bewitching
Captivating
Delighting
Enticing
Fascinating
Glowing
Harmonizing
Inspiring
Joyfulizing
Kissing
Loving
Mesmerizing
Naughtifying
Opening
Pampering
Queenly
Ravishing
Seducing
Tempting
Unveiling
Voluptuous
Wilding
XXX-Rated
Youthening
Zesty

Big Bang Blooming

Breathe in prana from the Air…

Breathe in mana from the Sea…

Breathe in Reiki from the Stars…

Breathe in life force from the Earth…

(yes, beloved, yes, breathe, yes, you, yes, here, yes, now…)

What if, everywhere you look and breathe and are, you are being embraced by a sacred sweetness that adores you?

What if, no matter what you think or say, no matter what you do or do not do, you are being held by a divine ancient matrix of Light?

What if, however you look or dress, however much money you have or don't have, no matter what anyone else thinks or speaks about you, you are more than enough and worthy of every blessing you could ever imagine—and more?

Can you choose to live … to be loved … in this YOUniverse?

Can you feel the Big Bang blooming in your holy heart?

Sage Taylor Kingsley

To Love with Hearts Wide Open

We are here to love with hearts wide open
embracing and embraced
with a love bigger than the world
with a love just how God loves us:
endless, timeless, formless.

What an INCREDIBLE GIFT
that all humans are built ~
divinely designed ~
to achieve this
to express this
to receive this
to live in full alignment as who we truly are.
Yet what a tragedy that so few of us do!

May these words open your heart's door
…. just …. that much … wider …

I Won't Groan Up

I finally figured out what I wanna be when I grow up: a poet! ('cept I *did* know it half a century ago but just sorta forgot it there for awhile) and, sure, maybe I have to impersonate a Responsible Adult *sometimes* but **I don't ever hafta be a groan-up** and you can't make me— nyahnyahnyahnyahnyah!

She Is Breathing

she is breathing
        the ocean is breathing
she is flowing
        the ocean is flowing
inbreath inflow
outbreath outflow

light dappling on dazzling waves
rays of sky turned to elixir
she breathes and we all live

she is breathing
        the ocean is breathing
she is healing
        the ocean is healing

all softness, surrendering remembrance
we came from her foamy breast
we bleed with her and her sister, Luna

she is breathing
        the ocean is breathing
she is love
        the ocean is love

cycles and spirals, swirls and eddies
currents and rivers, clouds and even
our sweat and tears
she breathes and all flows and lives

she is breathing
the ocean is breathing
she is living
the ocean is alive

Sage Taylor Kingsley

There's Beauty in This Booty

last day as a fiftysomething

yoga mat on urban emerald grass

heart kisses sky

~

today is a beautiful day, She whispers

today is your day

make it count, make it yours, make it shine

~

shakin' my magic booty to the four directions

blowing kisses to trees whose leaves blow them back

thumpin' my heart body drum

flirting with forever

Happy Mirthday!

Today is my birthday.
I'll make it a Mirth Day.
It's also Unearth Day.
A joyous Rebirth Day.
An Energy Surf Day.
Enjoying My Turf Day.
But perhaps most important:
Remember My Worth Day. ~Sage

(Written on my Big 6-Oh!!!)

When I Am 60

When I am 60

I will smell like

Patchouli and moonlight and lavender and sex.

Oh, wait, I already am.

Oh, great! I already do.

Tick Tock...

I'm measuring everything in time (how long ago did I start doing this?)
As if weeks, hours, minutes, and months were universal currencies
The tenant? 9 more weeks
That bottle of supplements? 10 days left
My weight? At goal by Valentine's
Neighbor? Love to walk with her next week
Work projects? I'm booking now for Q1 and Q2, solid for 3 months
Elderly mother? She has three years' worth of savings, at the rate she's burning through it
My living situation? First time living alone since 1997 (and that was only for 6 months) and before that it was 1986 (for a year). Now I've had Empty Nest for 18 days
New love? Maybe I'll be ready to date in 6 months, maybe in a year
I just can't seem to turn off this clock or set down the calendar
Is this symptomatic of my turning 60, now in my third third, this spinning and whizzing by faster and faster? My fancy new noise-canceling fancy earbuds won't silence the
tick tock, tick tock ...

Sage Taylor Kingsley

Through the Eyes of Beauty

Looking back on old photos
I see that sweet skinny little girl, her innocence, her playfulness, quiet,
books and bangs, and purple bike with sparkly handlebar streamers,
and I think: "I was so beautiful then, so adorable!"

(A voice whispers: *I am beautiful now*)

My teenage self, all 120 pounds of me, doing a photo shoot, black
permed big hair, bright red lipstick, flirty smile, my sister, eight years
older, took those photos in the hallway of our tiny apartment in
Queens, and these photos impressed Eileen Ford,
NYC's top fashion modeling agency,
I was beautiful, thin, confident, chic

(A voice whispers: *I am beautiful now*)

Me as a young mother, sweet smile, three year-old standing next
to me on my left, little baby in my lap, loving husband on my
right, JCPenney package deal, I'm wearing that Monet-inspired,
green-and-white dress echoing the spring backdrop. I was so beautiful
then, so full of love for my husband and children,
an embodiment of the Mother, creatrix, nurturer

(A voice whispers: *I am beautiful now*)

Beautiful Late Bloomer

In the spotlight, early 40s, speaking on a huge stage before 930 souls about radical self-love, in my power, the power of love. I was so beautiful, in my compassionate passion, bold, visible

(A voice whispers: *I am beautiful now*)

Today, my locks of silver … body differently abled, rounded, slower-paced, poet, wordsmith, homeowner, landlady, neighbor, caregiver, mother, daughter, friend, sister, dog mama, lover

I am beautiful now, the voice speaks calmly, clearly.

I am beautiful now.
I will always be beautiful.

SAGE TAYLOR KINGSLEY

Legs? Or Legacy?

I'm at an age where:

I worry less about a first impression … and more about a lasting impact.

I think less about
"Do I belong? Am I popular?" …
and more about "Am I being as loving as I can? Am I authentic?"

I focus less on my valuables …
and more on my values.

I yearn less for presents …
and more for presence.

And I care less about my legs …
and more about my legacy.

The Ghost in You

the ghost in you
seeks acclaim
untarnished
laments time wasted
whilst talents ticked by

that ghoulish dervish
shrieks and spins
strike now!
risk it all!
better to burn than dim and fade

that boddhisatva bantering
whispering the chorus of muses
panting behind your lidded veils
sees all your quantum youniverses
pokes   cajoles   tickles:
live it all, give it all

It's not too late—but wake up.
Please, please. The world is waiting

Sage Taylor Kingsley

When I Am an Old Woman ...

When I am an old woman,
sure, I'll still wear purple
and still say outrageous things courageously

... but what do I really want to do with my waning days?

I will keep shining, like the moon, whose crescent
silver sliver is all the more precious for her smaller stature.

I will garden and listen to birds more,
just randomly stopping and smiling at them
to thank them for reminding me life is a song.

I will write and read and live and breathe poetry.

I will spend less time on screens and more time in scenes.

I will gaze more at sunsets and moonrises and starshines.

I will care less about what people think
and more about how people feel.

I will get lost in the rapturous sacred geometry of flowers
and find myself there.

Yes, I will deliciously do less and bountifully be more.

What if I loved myself enough right now
to give myself these gifts of presence today?

Everything is aglow, inviting me, you, all of us,
to dance in this sacred revelry.

Join us.

~ Inspired by Jenny Joseph's "Warning"

Sage Taylor Kingsley

I Saw God Sitting on a Bench

I saw God sitting on a bench.

She had a sketchpad in her lap and a distant expression in her faraway eyes as her hand scribbled: madly, daintily, softly, boldly.

She was drawing a self-portrait, you see.

She turned the page and continued.

"What are you drawing?" I asked her.

"Everyone and everything I see," she said, turning another page.

I saw that next to her on the bench there were dozens of journals, I presumed already filled … or waiting to be graced by her art.

"Why do you need to draw us? Why draw all of this when it is already here?" I asked, curiously.

"I do not make art only to create," she said. "I make art to celebrate."

Just then, I heard music and saw that several people in the park were now playing a variety of instruments. Some of them were playing their own bodies as instruments, slapping thighs, pounding chests, snapping fingers. Some of them were banging garbage cans and clanging pot lids with spatulas.

The rhythm was infectious, delicious, and my feet began to move and my arms to sway and my mouth to laugh as the dance that had been waiting inside me began to tingle every cell of my body and the soles of my feet and my heart all at once. Ineffably, delectably.

"You see," said God, finally putting down Her pencil, "you are the art. Life is the dance. And the world around you is always singing."

Then she got up and held my hands and swung me around, and her head slinged back as we laughed at the clouds dancing with one another and tickling the birds' beaks.

So why are you still reading this?
Go dance.
Sing.
Make art.
Make love.

Make life a celebration, and you will see God on every bench, and hear Her in every song.

Sage Taylor Kingsley

Bloom and Shine!

It's never too late to bloom and to shine!
So don't you dare doubt and compare,
My dear, you're perfectly on time!

It's never too late to be who you are!
The YOUniverse needs your free verse
Your path is perfectly on par.

It's never too late to live a life full of bliss!
So use your voice and rejoice!
With Love as your guide, you can't miss.

It's never too late to turn your face toward the Light.
Your very presence is the essence
Bringing joy and delight.

It's never too late to bloom and to shine!
This is your hour, my sweet flower,
To boldly blossom—Divine.

Flower Power

There's something about sunflowers.

Their exuberant cheerfulness, exclaiming:
Turn toward the light! and
Aren't I lovely? So are you!
never feels excessive or showy,
just sparklymagical

Mandala smiles beaming

Perfect color scheme: Irish emerald leaves,
summer hill browns, and that yellow—oh!—that
orangey yellow that makes your heart leap

Swirling spirals
dancing like lovers
ascending forever inside DNA staircase

Those Golden Ratio-directed tasty seeds packed
with teeny proteiny perfection

Optimally arranged to receive photons from above,
earthy goodness from below

Sexiest
Fibonacci sequence ever.

If you count the number of clockwise and counterclockwise spirals in the seeds on the face of a sunflower, each number is the sum of the previous two such as 1, 2, 3, 5, 8, 13, 21, 34, 55, 89, 144, 233, 377, 610 ... or another Fibonacci irrational number sequence that theoretically continues forever. The sunflower's designer chose this mathematical arrangement to maximize how many seeds the flower can fuel and feed.

Or maybe She or He was just showing off.

Sage Taylor Kingsley

Yummilicious

People see my hair, my lines, they hear my age, and they assume, "Oh, she must be all dried up. Like a prune." Oh, honey, I am sweeter than a mango, tastier than an orange, juicier than a hot peach that drenches your chin while the Sun caresses your cheek. Oh, if only they knew! I am not a number of stellar revolutions. I am not bones and dust, not yet, not yet. I am a fuckalicious portal. And I know, finally, what I am: Ripe.

Aging

aging
and sageing
and turning the paging

gracefully
and gratefully
and kindly and graciously

seeing
and freeing
and most of all: Being.

~ Inspired by James Crews

Ageless

her hands are spotted
like the barn owl's wings
like the speckled orchids
like the ladybug's back

her face has lines
like the trunks of sequoias
like the streaks of storm clouds
like the layers of rocks marking time

her body has curves
like the ripples of pebble in pond
like the mountaintops caressed by sky
like the heavenly bodies ever dancing

she chooses to be her real self
no Botox no nipping no tucking
just a smile in the mirror
knowing her beauty is
ageless

When Was the Last Time...?

When was the last time:
- You thanked the Sun setting the world aglow, contemplative, complete, content?
- You greeted the Moon with arms wide open and halo crowned?
- You soared from star to star with your eyes, mind and spirit?

When was the last time:
- You locked eyes until time's veil slipped away?
- You linked arms and danced til you sank, spent, body happy, heart uplifted?
- You laughed so hard you lost your breath as you found your joy of living again?

When was the last time:
- You kissed "I love you" to every single inch of your glorious self?
- You tasted sweat, sex, skin, crying with the beauty of it all, walls dissolved in wildness and wetness and wonder?
- You heard your own voice in the dawn chorus as you sang the new world into being?

And when will be the last time?

Writing through the Ages...

When I was 20, writing was venting.
When I was 30, writing was exploring.
When I was 40, writing was visioning.
When I was 50, writing was healing.
Now I am 60, and writing is leaving a legacy.

The Treasure in the Mirror

your lovability
does not depend on
what you weigh or earn
or your zip code or age or, really,
anything that can ever be measured

your lovability
is only based on
the fact that you live
and breathe and learn and give
and strive to thrive with kindness
to share your glowing heart a'pleasured

your lovability
will only ever grow
as you more deeply know
you are worthy and wondrous
deservingly desirably delectable
destined to shine ever brighter where'e'er you go
smile assuredly for surely you forever are treasured

Sage Taylor Kingsley

Your Words Are Your Wonder

Your words are your wonder.
scribbles of ink on tree skin
Your words are your wonder.
seemingly random streamingly wanton
Your words are your wonder.
"Why this word and not that?" Pokes Monkey Mind
"Later. Write after blahblahblah," pipes Distractor.
"Nobody cares. Nobody listens. Nobody reads it. Why bother?"
pounds Critic.

And yet, ever, always, still, I know:
My Words Are My Wonder.

My way
My wisdom
My whimsy
My whys
My wows
My witchiness
My wit
<u>My</u> words
<u>My</u> wonder

So, go.

Write and speak and listen and blissen
and shine and sing and whisper and share
and tell your goddamn blessed story because
You're the ONLY ONE who can

Beautiful Late Bloomer

And the world needs your wonder
and your wonder
feeds
you.

Sage Taylor Kingsley

graysquishyoldishsoftstrongkissablefuckableGORGEOUS

My hair is so gray.
      Yes! So silvery & sparkly & shiny!
My skin shows veins, wrinkles,
freckles, and what are these red splotches??
      My skin is soft & supple.
      Every dot is another spot to kiss.
My eyes are a drab brown, too small. Boring.
    My deep soulful eyes richly range from dark
    olive to coffee, smoky, sensual, sacred.
      Portals to my emotions.

My tummy is too big. Squishy.
    My tummy is a comfortable pillow for my
    lover's happy head.
My legs are lumpy. Chubby.
    My long, strong legs powerfully root my
    trunk to my earth. Dancing, walking,
    wrapped around my wrapt amor. Sexy AF.
My body is oldish. Roundish. I will never look
like a sexy young hottie again.
    My body is a womanly temple. Miraculous!
    Mature. Magical. Ripe. Rhythmic. Horny.
    Healthy. Happy. Kissable. Fuckable. Lovable.

I AM A GORGEOUS GODDESS.

YOU: A Love Poem

You're not too old
You're not too poor
You're not too bold
You're not too pure

It's not too soon
It's not too late
For you to bloom
And celebrate

You're not alone
You are all one
Time to enthrone
This holy one

In flowing gown
Astride a star
The moon your crown
Love, who you are.

YONIverse

she's not the same

in her teens and twenties, she was all about the O

she made her clit smile three times a day, more regularly than she ate food

she was all about turning men's heads and raising their cocks

delighting in her newfound power

she even created "The World's Best Romantic Board Game for Lovers"
... *Passion Play!*
(so said *The Playboy Catalogue*)

she had threesomes, drank and smoked too much, ate too many chicken wings, she was all about the pleasure

her sexually creative marriage ran its course in just a few years (but the whipped cream and whip were oh so fun)

in her thirties she played sex roulette: black white young old male female

~ ~ ~ exploring ~ ~ ~

then she married a sweet man whose cock stayed asleep for decades

in her forties she went into a sad cave

Beautiful Late Bloomer

she slid there
she hid there
she cried there
she died there

a long
slow
lonely
death
of
passion

then one day

another divorce
and many years and tears later
                                          she healed
she healed more
she healed deeper
she healed stronger

she felt stirrings

they reminded her of a baby's quickening, flutters and the feeling of aliveness again, the surprise of feeling anything, anything at all "down there"

moons passed

                                    suns rose

and one day she burst into flames
soaked by her own amrita
and sweat and coming
fire and water
awake

Sage Taylor Kingsley

alive
aware
anew

all at once
the goddess' yoni opened up devoured her spat her out into a realm of
bliss she never even knew
existed

lying in wonder upon drenched sheets she asked *what was this flood?*
heard the word: *amrita* whispered softly

and she knew

she knew she would never again lock her kundalini in a cave
she tasted herself and knew her body's fountain of youth was
wholly holy

she knew the right partner would arrive on goddess time
to pray with ~ play with ~ lay with

in her fifties she was all about balance and flow, ecstasy and presence,
expansion and surrender

and now
in full bloom

she says yes to her goddessence

she knows all the pleasures and treasures of the Yoniverse are hers

PART III

BLISSING

Bask

bask...
feel the lovelight
the Earthmother holding you close
the stellar radiance imbuing you with vibrance, brilliance

fill...
the heart's cup with gratitude
the breath of the ancestors chanting deep wholeness, holiness in your
bones

linger...
in the ocean of trust and time
in the gift of self-worthiness, bestowed, remembered

drink...
in the nectarous lush amrita
in the sweet medicine of the now

Sage Taylor Kingsley

The Invitation

The Infinite Force and Source of All Love in the Universe (and YOUniverse) invites you.
To declare.
To climax.
To dance.
To sculpt.
To savor.
To laugh.
To paint.
To write.
To glow.
To play.
To spin.
To rest.
To kiss.
To frolic.
To drink.
To soften.
To caress.
To surrender.
To begin again.

This is the BEST INVITATION you will ever receive!

How do you RSVP yes to reserve your space?
I have more good news, God news for you!

Beautiful Late Bloomer

Your space is already, all ready, reserved.
Your invitation is unlimited.
You have a special place at the banquet table.

Your namecard, with your name in glitter, is placed at the seat of honor.
And the playlist? All your favorites.
Best of all, you can party as hard, or as soft, as you like and will never get a hangover. Just a lovedallover.

Join me, join us.
It's party time!
I can't wait to dance with you.

~ Inspired by akasha
(whose book Love Everything *I had the divine pleasure of editing)*

Poets Sure Know How to Throw Great Orgies (Wanna Come?)

I am the love child offspring from that crazy orgy between Maya, Anais, Henry, Walt, Oscar, Pablo, Mary, the other Henry, Hildegard, Rumi, and Rupi.

Peach Sunrises

I am remembering…

peach sunrises gulls' cries Atlantic shores
bundling up in hat, scarf, and coat tossed out of trunk my first day in
California, beach parking lot. August.

sheep with neon green, pink, blue butts getting lost roadside in
Ireland, hilarious rescue attempt, huge gaps in every fence

gazing, astonished, as lava dripped into sea and new land shaped,
sizzling, steaming, glowing red hot

cacophonous raucous chickens squawking dozen dogs barking tropical
unnamed birds my Balinese alarm clock

thirty dolphins playing with our kayak's wake, baby the length of my
forearm shimmying tip-to-tail at apogee: I'm alive!!! I'm alive!!!

soft cool mossy trunks, ferns and fronds, there is no sweeter silence
than forest's green

I am remembering to remember
to bow to it All, kissing moon and earth, cloud and
star with my grateful tears

Deeper and Deeper

the deeper I surrender
to the calm
floating in eternity's awareness
embraced embracing
the center
the new
the now
the always

the deeper into stillness I go
the more my soul wants to dance
in utter stillness
I spin
following the orbits of the heavenly
bodies
every axis
vertical horizontal temporal ineffable
all meeting in the one point
the oneness
the wonder
the heart
this tiny infinite heart of mine
that is the Beloved's

the deeper I turn my gaze
to the calm to the cool to the cave
the brighter the One Sun shines!
inward
caressing the mystery

Beautiful Late Bloomer

godward
finding You
traveling farther
crossing galaxy's rims

the deeper I listen to the silence
the sweeter the song of the spheres
the clearer the dulcet tones of the I Am
whispering my true name

deeper
here
in no thing
I find
All

deeper
here
in no naming
I find

the eternal dance
with my forever
lover

the poem
that never
ends

Sage Taylor Kingsley

See the Love in All Things

Once you See

the Love

in all things

you can never

go back to

un-Seeing.

Thank goodness!

Thank Godness!

Thank Goddessness!

So go ahead.

Look in the mirror.

~ *Inspired by Helen Keller*

Efflorescence

A phosphorescence
Of liminal luminosity
An effervescence
Of kundalini bubbling
A luminescence
Of inner radiance
A deliquescence
Of liquid love
A revirescence
Of youthening nectars
An opalescence
Of soul's light reflected
A rejuvenescence
Of life's eternal hum
An efflorescence
Of the bloom eternal.

Sage Taylor Kingsley

I Will No Longer Tolerate Itchy Sweaters!

I will no longer tolerate rough tags
or itchy sweaters irritating my soft neck
or too-tight too-pointy shoes pinching my sweet feet
or not-quite-right-for-me(-anymore) relationships
or my-soul-is-dying-here jobs
or homes that don't feel like home
or foods that don't nourish me
or "entertainment" that weighs me down and taints my gorgeous
fucking aura.

Nope. Not anymore.

We, as women, have been conditioned to ignore
the crucial messages from our bodies and psyches and our dreams and
the Moon and

We, as women, accepted the insidious unconscious training to
wait, to
take care of everyone and everything else, first, and so
our time, our turn, never
comes.

So. Today. I. Stopped.

I stopped all that nonsense and I took off my shirt and
I cut. Out. That. Itchy. Damn. Tag.
and I smiled as I
threw
OUT!

Beautiful Late Bloomer

all that bullshit right along with that tag
and
instead
I picked up this pen
and I wrote this
love poem
to you.

Sage Taylor Kingsley

go ahead, be self-bliss

It's not selfish to love yourself.
It's self-BLISS.

Once

this glorious gorgeous day
shining your precious eyes open
only comes once

this miraculous magical moonlight
beaming streaming gleaming
upon your holy crown
only shines now

this splendid surprising starlight
that has been traveling to you for years, decades, centuries
perhaps from a star long gone
is a gift to you
only right now

this soft soothing breath
restoring your vitality and lifeforce
releasing all you no longer need
only happens here, now
in your breast, in your chest
feel this

this raw aliveness
this divine blissness
this remembrance of your joy
this reclaiming of your essence
this sacred treasure that is you
only comes
once

Sage Taylor Kingsley

A Liminal Luminosity

a liminal luminosity

a soft surrender

a dropping of doingness

when we embrace the void
we find ourselves embraced

graced

held in Love's warm lap
She kisses our crown tenderly

auric glitter tingling
the delicate fibers of our skin
reweave stardust

until we find our feet on
Mother's rich humus again

glimmering from within

~ Inspired by Arielle Ford

when did we forget we are animals?

when did we forget we are animals?

was it when electric lights tricked us out of our natural rhythms?

when did we forget we are built for sensation, for sensuality, for touch, for tenderness?

was it when we bought the lie that our flesh needed to be hidden at all times, that skin is a sin?

when did we forget we have feet?

was it when we became obsessed with thinking, cut off at the necks, and sublimated the sublime gift of softly being?

when did we forget we were designed for ecstasy?

was it when Eve was framed and shamed and blamed for acting on her desire?

when did we forget the everyday miracle of breath and bone and blood?

was it when we abandoned our joy?

when did we forget we are beautiful?

Sage Taylor Kingsley

The Heart's Camera

The most beautiful moments are never captured by a camera

The most wonderful sights are never cast on a canvas

The most soothing sounds are never recorded with little boxes or buttons

The most blissful feelings are never contained by ten thousand poets scribbling, scrabbling as all alchemists do while hearing the secret clock tick

The most graceful dances are never choreographed or rehearsed

The most tender of treasures are fleetest of foot

ephemeral
personal
magical
ineffable
immeasurable

at once external and internal
eternal

slippery like tadpoles in a pond
transforming before our eyes
gone before our breath comes back to our astonished chests

where we gasp

completely filled
completely emptied

but the heart camera
clicked

it remembers

if we awaken into but one moment like this
our soul will celebrate it forever
rippling joy's song on soul's pond

touch your heart now
eyes closed or open
gaze farther
inward or outward
tap that center
feel the pulse of life's wordless wonderment

Sage Taylor Kingsley

You Are Forever a Mother

I don't care if your children are themselves parents or grandparents,
you are forever a mother.

I don't care your only child has crossed the great divide, or only drew a few breaths, you are forever a mother.

I don't care if you were only pregnant long enough to get that positive test, or to feel the slightest butterfly tickles in your belly,
you are forever a mother.

I don't care if you have never birthed any human babies, and all of your children have fur or feathers or scales, you are forever a mother.

I don't care if your birdlings, nourished for 18, 20, 30 years, have flown the nest and now you're trying to figure out who you are when you're not so focused on being a mother,
you are forever a mother.

I don't care if the child that came from your womb was raised by another woman whose name you never spoke aloud, whose hand you never held, you are forever a mother.

I don't care if the child you birthed does not contain your genetic material but by some magic streamed forth from your womb with a great sigh, you are forever a mother.

I don't care if the child you raised so tenderly was another mother's first, for however short a time.

And the only lie in all of this is this: *I do care.*

I care a great deal. I care about all the mothers. I care about how the mothers were mothered. I care about how the mothers mother themselves. I care about healing the generational trauma and blessing our lineage all the way back to First Mother, so we can all, finally, lay down all the burdens. I care about Mother Earth, the Great Mother of All Life. And I care about all those who care for and care about the mothers, and that means you.

May you forever know
your worth.

May the infinite unconditional love of the Divine Mother kiss your brow, fill you with the sweet creamy elixir of life itself, hold you gently, and sing love songs to you while we all dream a new world into being.

Love Activation #1

Let Love be my power.
Love is my power.

Let Light be my guidepost.
Light is my guidepost.

Let Passion be my playground.
Passion is my playground.

Let Truth be my voice.
Truth is my voice.

Let Kindness be my choice.
Kindness is my choice.

Let Now be my portal.
Now is my portal.

Cracking Open the Heart Egg

When our heart egg cracks open,
at first
it may feel like a breaking
an aching…

But the thin shell around our tender heart
was neither dropped nor smashed.
Love is not violent, dramatic,
uncalled for.

Love is more gradual, miraculous.
Sought. Bidden.

Our tender heart needed to expand.
This was all timed perfectly,
all this pecking and poking at our calcified boundaries.

Our stronger, older, wiser, heart bird
sets itself free
gazes, stretches, smiles…

Flies.

So when you feel yourself cracking
open
just
trust
because your little heart bird knows
exactly what it's doing.

She Is Remembering

she is remembering
her wholeness
her holiness

she is whispering
wind's wisdom
in her own inner ear

she is laughing
at the daffodils' endless faith
at the wonder of it all

she is becoming
the one she ever has been
the one she most admires and cherishes

she is forgetting
whatever was keeping her enchained
whatever song of amnesia had stolen her enchantments

she is allowing herself
the grace to do nothing
the strength to be everything

she is holding
the treasure box in her chest
the one she gifted herself
long ago, and tomorrow

Beautiful Late Bloomer

she is blowing kisses
above, below, and all around
and most of all, in the mirror

she is drinking deep
of the cosmic mother's milk
of the amrita of eternity

she is reclaiming
every wood witch, every sprite
every dragon, crow, and wolf

she is nurturing and nurtured
true abundance is her feast
truth to power her path home

Sage Taylor Kingsley

Sturdy Star Stuff

I am made of sturdy star stuff

Star stuff
Earthy stuff

I am the primordial gossamer goddess.

I am the Big Bang
Over and over
A million bajillion infinitillion Big Bangs in my body
Every cell wise

I am the earthy birthday mirthy flirty
Kissable caressable deliciousization of your dreams

I remember who I am now

Now

I k-NOW who I am

What I want
What I deserve
What I desire

I dance into this creation
Elation
Womanifestation
Celebration!

I cocreate Elationships

I embody inbody Life Force Light Source Love Force
On course
Of course
Awesome sauce

I am made of sturdy stuff

I AM

All
That
IS

I AM

Earth and Heaven
Moon and Sun
In cosmic embrace and grace and everyplace

I AM

Everywhere and Everywhen
I stand strong in my power
My name and claim my fame
I empower myself in the Love I AM
YES!

Health is my birthright
Prosperity is my birthright
Happiness is my birthright
Health, prosperity and happiness are MY CHOICE

    My destiny
               My reality
                  My truth

    I remember this
    I remember bliss

      I remember
        Who
         I
        AM.

The Ecstasy of Being

The only way to love yourself is wholly, holy, radiantly, radically ... blowing astonishingly tender kisses to the divine crone-child in the mirror.

The only way to tolerate the soul-crushing weight of the world's pain is altruistically, alchemically, transmuting the agony of suffering into acts of kindness, prayers of hope, and many moments of microscopic gratitude.

The only way to feel comfort's grace wrapping around this aging form, this slowly crumbling temple of yours, of yearning, is to celebrate, lavishly, ravishingly, the miraculous fucking fact that you ever existed at all, that somehow your heartbrain knows everything and nothing, that your eyes catch starfire that's not even there, that you walk around, a sack made 70% of water, discussing poetry and politics and passion and the price of pomegranates like it's nothing when in fact, my dear, *this*—you, me, this! single breath—is everything.

The only way this poem will ever end is when we live the ecstasy of being so completely, complicitly, deliciously, delightedly: we become the poem, crumbling and shining in erotic entropy, one sigh, one song, one smile at a time.

Sage Taylor Kingsley

On the Altar of Her Becoming

on the altar
of her becoming
she had placed herself
supine
aligned with the rising sun
and setting moon

she had placed other offerings:
crystals of tourmaline rose and quartz
petals of calendula rose and jasmine
branches and bundles of sage and sweetgrass

adorning
adoring

now she lay there
expecting the magic she had summoned
knowing that Heaven and Earth
desired her healing
desired her healed
as much as she did
and more so much more

and they gathered around her:
the witches and fairies
the wolves and dragons
the dryads and nyads
the medicine women and muses
the angels and ancestors

Beautiful Late Bloomer

adorning
adoring

they lay their magic upon her:
the oils and potions
the dust and glitter
the kisses and caresses
the winds and waters
they spun tales and backwards ran the clock

she had cried
kneeling before the marble stone:
heal me!
that I may heal with your words
in this world and in all the worlds
guide me!
that I may be your hands and voice
in this world and in all the worlds
illuminate me!
that I may be your light
in this world and in all the worlds

heard and held and healed
she opened her eyes
It was all just a dream, wasn't it?
But, oh, what a beautiful dream!

And the Goddess smiled
and the goddess smiled

adorned
adored
always

The Right One for You

The right one for you
gives you tender kisses on your back and shoulder and all over
Just because

The right one for you is just as filled and fulfilled gazing into your eyes
as being astride you because his soul dances inside you

Fully present with you, the right one for you doesn't compare you
to other women because you go so far beyond what he has ever
experienced, there is no comparison

The right one for you feels like the luckiest man in the world, and tells
you this often with the deepest sincerity, respect and gratitude

The right one for you can bring you to the brink of ecstasy and
beyond with the slightest touch of his fingertips or tongue, and brings
you to your knees, eager to please him and return the favor with savor

The right one for you worships you, body, mind, heart and soul, as the
Goddess you truly are

The right one for you owns when he strays off his path, apologizes,
and while he is not perfect, does his best to honor his agreements, and
he always speaks his truth

The right one for you provides a safe haven in his loving arms for all of
the wounded parts of you

Beautiful Late Bloomer

The right one for you plays with giddy abandon with your inner child

The right one for you becomes a wild animal with your sensual, primal, lusty self, and brings out the wild creature in heat within your flesh

The right one for you heeds the sage counsel of the wise woman within you

The right one for you knows when to lead you and when to follow you, because he always walks by your side as your equal

The right one for you sees you, hears you, inspires you, reveres you, and sanctifies you beyond what you ever dreamed possible

The right one for you feels like home.

SAGE TAYLOR KINGSLEY

Softly, a Love Note

Softly,
a love note
singing
soaring

From that place where all magic comes from

Into mind and heart and breath

Dancing along arm and into delighted fingers

Landing,
softly,
everywhere.

Eternity in Your Eyes

eternity in your eyes
forever in your kiss
surrender in your sighs
ascension in your bliss

ever dancing in your arms
ever bathing in your glow
ever rising in your charms
ever swimming in your flow

take my hand in sweet caress
take my heart into your soul
take my side and effervesce
in your love I found my home

Sage Taylor Kingsley

Dancing Love Bubbles

I.

The love in me dances
with the love
in you

The love in you dances
with the love
in me

We embrace
and
are embraced

We enchant
and
are enchanted

We reflect
We remind
We restore
We recall
We renew
We revive
We rejoice!

II.

We're not just in a Love Bubble.
Love bubbles are in us!
Best champagne ever made.

III.

Be love,
Beloved.

IV.

Wash (your whole essence with Love Shampoo!)
Rinse (away anything and everything that is not love)
Repeat (this is what it's *really* all about, not the Hokey Pokey!)

V.

YES!!! I can see your sparkly dancing Love bubbles from here!
Oh wait! We ARE the sparkly dancing Love bubbles! Wheeeee!!!!

pat pat pat

pat pat pat
means
I love you

taught this to my beloved
as a secret love message
pat pat pat
on his thigh

lying in bed now
pat pat pat
on my own heart

giver and receiver
sweet Morse code of adoration
that needs no alphabet or translation

pat pat pat
feel that?
that one was for YOU

We Interrupt This Poetry Book to Bring You an Important Message from Your Creator

You are Light.
You are Divine.
You are good
And you are worthy.

And above all:
YOU ARE LOVE.

When I said:
Let there be Light,
Who do you think I was talking about?

Sage Taylor Kingsley

Worship the Hands

Worship the hands
Worship with the hands

Kiss your beloved's fingertips
Kiss the palms
Kiss the base of the wrist

Caress the knuckles
Think of how these hands pleasure you
Celebrate how these hands create in the world

Worship the hands
Worship with the hands

Hold one hand at a time
between both your ardent palms

Breathe love into these hands
These holy, gentle hands
These soft, strong hands

Worship the hands
Worship with the hands

Hold your beloved's hand
like brand-new lovers
discovering one another

Beautiful Late Bloomer

Hold your beloved's hand
like the long-married couple
knowing each other's thoughts

Worship the hands
Worship with the hands

Kiss the back of the hands
Place the thumb in your mouth
Swirl and tongue and suck and tantalize

Create deep surrender within your beloved
Allow their soul to be graced through their hands
Place their hand over your heart
Your hand over theirs

Worship the hands
Worship with the hands

These soft, gentle hands of love

Sage Taylor Kingsley

I No Longer Pray . . .

I no longer pray with books
I pray with brooks

I no longer pray at churches
I pray at beaches

I no longer pray in rows
I pray in groves

I no longer pray with priests
I pray with feasts

I no longer pray on hard wooden benches
I pray on soft mossy boulders

I no longer pray on Sundays
I pray to moonbeams and sun rays

I no longer pray for salvation
I pray through celebration

I no longer pray bowing to rules
I pray riding on rainbows

I no longer pray to placate God's authority
I pray to express Love's priority

I no longer pray out of guilt
I pray into gratitude

Beautiful Late Bloomer

I no longer pray to find my way to heaven
I pray to keep my heart open on Earth

When every moment has become a prayer
no prayer is required.

~ Inspired by Chelan Harkin's "I No Longer Pray"

Sage Taylor Kingsley

As If

Life is short
Write and speak as if the world depends upon your wisdom
Because it does

Dream as if anything can be yours
Because it can

Act as if all you do makes a difference
Because it does and you do

Treat yourself as if you are a precious treasure
Because you are

Smile as if Joy is your birthright
Because it is

Be brave, feel peaceful and inspired
As if you just remembered everything that truly matters
Because you did

Live as if Love is everything
Because it is

Just. One. More.

just one more,
I beg the masters

pierce my heart
make me bleed words of Love
again and again
until all the world
feels these rebirth pangs as I do

we are all the chosen ones
our brows the wombs

push! says the midwife
kiss the head
count the toes

a breath
a moment of glory

then do it again
just one more

SAGE TAYLOR KINGSLEY

When Does It Ever End?

When does it ever end?
This astonishment every time I remember
the ecstasy of being

"When does it ever end?"
you ask, beloved

There is no ending when the remembering itself
is the beginning of forever

ABOUT THE POET

Sage Taylor Kingsley is a best-selling author, mystic and romantic poet who lives, breathes, eats, drinks, and dreams of poetry. She serves as a book doctor, editor, and ghostwriter (angelwriter ☺) at **Reedsy.com** and freelance at her own company: **Sage for Your Page.** Under her previous business, Prosperous Goddess[R], Sage provided intuitive life coaching, hypnotherapy, Reiki and meditation trainings, mother wound healing sessions, and spiritual retreats to thousands of awakening souls. Her Law of Attraction course, Angelic Abundance Activator, was voted the #1 manifestation program worldwide. Sage has written poetry for over half a century and has generated over 1,500 poems since 2021.

While this is her debut poetry collection, Sage's essays and poems have been featured in many books and bestsellers: *A New Season: Poems for a World in Flux* (edited by Jacalyn Eyvonne and Kathleen Herrmann); *Orange is Not a Colour: Poems Against Totalitarianism* (edited by Fin Hall); *Feisty! Dangerously Amazing Women Using Their Voices and Making an Impact* (edited by Sierra Melcher), winner of the 2024 Literary Titan Book Award; *Embraced by the Divine: The Emerging Woman's Gateway to Power, Passion, and Purpose* (edited by Michelle Mayur)*; Self-Caring* (by Michelle Peck), and *We'Moon Datebook*. She is also co-author of a science-fiction novel: *The Princess Key* (by Rick Clogston). Sage's music album, *Songs of Light,* is available on Spotify. Back in the 1990s, she co-created *Passion Play!*—acclaimed as "The best romantic board game ever made," by *The Playboy Catalogue*. She co-hosted *The Sexy and Sacred Show* podcast with Steve Gibbs, an award-winning nature photographer.

Originally from Queens, NYC, Sage raised two kind-hearted, smart young men and has called Northern California home for over two decades. She always has at least one dog, several jars of salsa and olives, and a ridiculous amount of tea in her house.

Beautiful Late Bloomer: Passionate Poetry and Mystic Musings is the first book of sacred, spicy, and sometimes sassy poetry in the Yoni-Verse™ series. (At least) Ten more poetry books are coming!

CONNECT WITH SAGE

Substack ~ Join her growing, glowing community there!
Check out Sage's blog, daily Love Notes & subscribe to her museletter at:
sagepoetess.substack.com ~ Museletter
substack.com/@sagepoetess ~ Profile

Link Tree with Facebook, IG, YouTube, Linked In, and free re-Sources:
https://linktr.ee/sagetheprosperousgoddess

Need a loving midwife for your book baby?
Sage specializes in curating and gently editing poetry,
editing and ghostwriting non-fiction (self-help and memoirs),
and editing science-fiction and fantasy.
She has been accused of turning manuscripts into masterpieces.
www.SageforYourPage.com

You can read reviews of Sage's editorial work at:
Reedsy.com/sage-taylor-kingsley
sagepoetess@gmail.com

If you were touched by these words of love, please consider:

- Gifting a copy of this book to someone you love.
- Sharing the link to the book, Substack, or website.
- Leaving a review on Amazon to boost the book's visibility.
- Donating a copy to a library, women's or homeless shelter, community or spiritual center.

Thank you so much!

Brightest Blessings and Blissings!
xo Sage ♥

www.ingramcontent.com/pod-product-compliance
Lightning Source LLC
Chambersburg PA
CBHW030327080526
44584CB00012B/751